ONE NATION,

HONORS *those who* SERVE

ONE NATION,

HONORS
*those who* SERVE

This book was written by Walnut Grove Press for exclusive use by the Popular Publishing Company.

Popular Publishing Company LLC
1700 Broadway
New York, NY 10019

ISBN 1-59027-065-7

*The ideas expressed in this book are not, in all cases, exact quotations, as some have been edited for clarity and brevity. In all cases, the author has attempted to maintain the speaker's original intent. In some cases, material for this book was obtained from secondary sources, primarily print media. While every effort was made to ensure the accuracy of these sources, the accuracy cannot be guaranteed. For additions, deletions, corrections or clarifications in future editions of this text, please write Popular Publishing Company LLC.*

Certain elements of this text, including quotations, stories, and selected groupings of Bible verses, have appeared, in part or in whole, in publications produced by Walnut Grove Press of Nashville, TN; these excerpts are used with permission.

Scripture taken from THE MESSAGE. Copyright © 1993, 1994, 1995, 1996. Used by permission of NavPress Publishing Group.

All scripture quotations, unless otherwise indicated, are taken from the HOLY BIBLE, NEW INTERNATIONAL VERSION ©. NIV ©. Copyright © 1973, 1978, 1984, by International Bible Society. Used by permission of Zondervan Publishing House. All rights reserved.

Scripture quotations marked (NLT) are taken from The Holy Bible, New Living Translation, Copyright © 1996. Used by permission of Tyndale House Publishers, Incorporated, Wheaton, Illinois 60189. All rights reserved.

Printed in the United States of America
Page Layout Design by Bart Dawson
Cover Design: Tiffany Berry

1 2 3 4 5 6 7 8 9 10 • 02 03 04 05 06 07 08 09 10

# TABLE OF CONTENTS

This grand experiment that is our American democracy has, on countless occasions, been tested in the crucible of history. In the beginning, men with familiar names like Washington, Jefferson, and Franklin patched together a fledgling nation. Less than a hundred years later, that nation divided against itself in a terrible conflict that claimed the lives of more of its soldiers than all other American wars combined. But America survived.

In the first years of the 20th century, the winds of war blew hot and fierce across the European continent. The War to End All Wars brought worldwide carnage, but it didn't end war. A generation after World War I, on a sunny December morning in 1941, Old Glory was dealt a staggering blow at Pearl Harbor, but the brave sons and daughters of America rose up as one and saved not only their nation but also the world.

In faraway places like Korea and Vietnam, in distant lands that many can scarcely name, America's best and bravest have carried the banner of freedom, fought for it, and sometimes died for it. And, they continue to do so today.

This book pays tribute to those who protect the American dream. These dedicated men and women serve in a variety of ways: military, police, firefighting, and healthcare, to name a few. Sometimes, their service takes them thousands of miles from home, and sometimes they're right next door. But, wherever they happen to be, however they choose to serve, we, as grateful Americans, thank them.

On September 11, 2001, America was once again tested by forces that would seek to destroy her. But as before, this generation of Americans stands ready to defend—and pass on—the precious liberties that are the legacy of their forefathers. Because of those who serve us and protect us, the Dream will live.

★ ★ ★ ★ ★

CHAPTER 1

★ ★ ★ ★ ★

# THE AMERICAN DREAM

The future belongs to those
who believe in the beauty
of their dreams.

ELEANOR ROOSEVELT

★　★　★　★　★

In a difficult and dangerous world, the American dream is alive and well. America remains a land of freedom, prosperity, and opportunity. It is a place where dreams can still come true for those who are willing to work hard and smart. It is still the world's great superpower, the world's great economic engine, and the world's great melting pot.

We Americans are blessed beyond measure. Of course, our nation is not perfect, but it remains the least imperfect nation on earth. And, as grateful citizens, we must do our part to protect America and preserve her liberties just as surely as we work to create better lives for ourselves and for our families.

The future of America depends upon those who serve and protect her; because of these courageous men and women, we Americans can dream . . . and we do.

I believe in America because we have great dreams and because we have the opportunity to make those dreams come true.

WENDELL WILKIE

The young do not know enough to be prudent, and therefore they attempt the impossible and achieve it, generation after generation.

PEARL BUCK

Sometimes people call me an idealist. Well, that is the way I know I am an American. America is the only idealistic nation in the world.

WOODROW WILSON

The history of every country begins in the heart of a man or woman.

WILLA CATHER

We hold these truths to
be self-evident, that all men
are created equal, that they are
endowed by their Creator with
certain unalienable rights, that
among these are Life, Liberty,
and the pursuit of Happiness.

THOMAS JEFFERSON

Dreams pass into the reality of action. From the action stems the dream again; and this interdependence produces the highest living.

ANAÏS NIN

I have learned this at least by my experiment; that if one advances confidently in the direction of his dreams, and endeavors to live the life he has imagined, he will meet with a success unexpected in common hours.

HENRY DAVID THOREAU

Ideas must work through the brains and the arms of good and brave people, or they are no better than dreams.

RALPH WALDO EMERSON

You can dream, create, design, and build the most wonderful place in the world, but it requires people to make the dream a reality.

WALT DISNEY

I like dreams of the future better than the history of the past.

THOMAS JEFFERSON

Twenty years from now you will be more disappointed by the things you didn't do than by the ones you did do. So throw off the bowlines. Sail away from the safe harbor. Catch the trade winds in your sails. Explore. Dream. Discover.

MARK TWAIN

Far away in the sunshine are my highest aspirations. I may not reach them, but I can look up and see the beauty, believe in them and try to follow where they lead.

LOUISA MAY ALCOTT

Nothing happens unless first a dream.

CARL SANDBURG

For this is what America is all about. It is the uncrossed desert and unclimbed ridge. It is the star that is not reached and the harvest that is sleeping in the unplowed ground.

LYNDON BAINES JOHNSON

Here is not merely a nation but a teeming nation of nations.

WALT WHITMAN

America was established not to create wealth but to realize a vision, to realize an ideal, to discover and maintain liberty among men.

WOODROW WILSON

America is essentially a dream, a dream as yet unfulfilled. It is a dream of a land where men of all races, of all nationalities, and of all creeds can live together as brothers.

MARTIN LUTHER KING, JR.

I do believe we shall continue to grow, to multiply and prosper until we exhibit an association powerful, wise, and happy beyond what has yet been seen.

THOMAS JEFFERSON

The idealists and visionaries, foolish enough to throw caution to the winds and express their ardor and faith in some supreme deed, have advanced mankind and have enriched the world.

EMMA GOLDMAN

Live out your imagination, not your history.

STEPHEN COVEY

Since it doesn't cost a dime to dream, you'll never shortchange yourself when you stretch your imagination.

ROBERT SCHULLER

S he presides over the New York Harbor, torch in hand, as both a symbol of international friendship *and* a physical manifestation of the American Dream. She is, of course, the Statue of Liberty, a gift from the people of France. And, when President Grover Cleveland accepted the statue on behalf of the United States on October 28, 1886, he said: "We will not forget that Liberty has here made her home; nor shall her chosen altar be neglected."

The familiar inscription on the statue is a testament to the promise of America:

*Give me your tired, your poor, Your huddled masses yearning to breathe free, The wretched refuse of your teeming shore. Send these, the homeless, tempest-tossed to me. I lift my lamp beside the golden door.*

On the occasion of the statue's fiftieth anniversary, Franklin D. Roosevelt said, "Millions of men and women adopted this homeland because in this land they found a home in which the things they most desired could be theirs—freedom of opportunity, freedom of thought, and freedom to worship God. Here they found life because here there was freedom to live. It is fitting, therefore, that this should be a service of rededication to the liberty and the peace which this statue symbolizes. Liberty and peace are living things. In each generation—if they are to be maintained—they must be guarded and vitalized anew."

This, generation, too, must protect the freedoms we hold dear. May we do so with courage, wisdom, perseverance, and faith.

It is never too late to dream or start something new.

LUCI SWINDOLL

One can never consent to creep when one has the impulse to soar.

HELEN KELLER

Too many people put their dreams "on hold." It takes an uncommon amount of guts to put your dreams on the line, to hold them up and say, "How good or bad am I?" That's where the courage comes in.

— ERMA BOMBECK

★ ★ ★ ★ ★
CHAPTER 2
★ ★ ★ ★ ★

# THE SPIRIT OF GENEROSITY

Turning our eyes to other
nations, our great desire is to
see our brethren of the human
race secured in the blessings
enjoyed by ourselves, and
advancing in knowledge,
in freedom, and
in social happiness.

ANDREW JACKSON

We Americans are richly blessed. We live in a prosperous, freedom-loving country; we are free to pursue the American Dream in a land of endless opportunities and countless second chances; we can worship God as we see fit and speak our minds as our consciences dictate—all without the fear of governmental reprisal.

As a prosperous nation, America has much to share with needy people the world over. And, of course, charity begins here at home. We Americans serve best when we serve those who cannot help themselves. To do so is to share a portion of the blessings that God *and* our forebears so generously shared with us.

We cannot live only for ourselves. A thousand fibers connect us with our fellow men.

HERMAN MELVILLE

The impersonal government can never replace the helping hand of a neighbor.

HUBERT H. HUMPHREY

I must admit that I personally measure success in terms of the contributions an individual makes to her or his fellow human beings.

MARGARET MEAD

Would we hold liberty, we must have charity; charity to others, charity to ourselves.

LEARNED HAND

Give what you have. To someone, it may be better than you dare to think.

HENRY WADSWORTH LONGFELLOW

The reward of a good deed is to have done it.

ELBERT HUBBARD

Assistance to the weak makes one strong. Oppression of the unfortunate makes one weak.

BOOKER T. WASHINGTON

Speak up for those who cannot speak for themselves, for the rights of all who are destitute.

PROVERBS 31:8 NIV

What is serving God? 'Tis doing good to man.

POOR RICHARD'S ALMANAC

We find in life exactly what we put in it.

RALPH WALDO EMERSON

If you haven't any charity in your heart, you have the worst kind of heart trouble.

BOB HOPE

There is a very real relationship, both quantitatively and qualitatively, between what you contribute and what you get out of this world.

OSCAR HAMMERSTEIN II

From what we get, we can make a living; what we give, however, makes a life.

ARTHUR ASHE

The good person is generous and lends lavishly....

PSALM 112:5 MSG

The influence of each human being on others in this life is a kind of immortality.

JOHN QUINCY ADAMS

When in need, ask. When in doubt, give.

MARIE T. FREEMAN

You can't hold a man down without staying down with him.

BOOKER T. WASHINGTON

Become genuinely interested in other people.

DALE CARNEGIE

We awaken in others the same attitude of mind we hold toward them.

ELBERT HUBBARD

Do unto others 20% better than you would expect them to do unto you to correct for subjective error.

LINUS PAULING

The best way to try to cheer yourself up is to try to cheer somebody else up.

MARK TWAIN

Happiness is a perfume that
you cannot pour on others
without getting a few drops
on yourself.

RALPH WALDO EMERSON

New York City was a far different place in the early 1900's when young Dale Carnegie began teaching courses on enthusiasm and salesmanship. Those courses are still offered today, and Carnegie's classic book, *How to Win Friends and Influence People*, remains a perennial best seller. Dale Carnegie's formula for success was straightforward: he advised, "Become genuinely interested in other people."

Ben Franklin would have agreed. Franklin observed, "A man wrapped up in himself makes a very small package." Indeed, self-absorption is not only a surefire way to shrink one's soul; it is also a proven prescription for unhappiness. But, when we look *outside* ourselves and become genuinely concerned for the well-being of others, we do them *and* ourselves an enduring service.

The highest test of the civilization of any race is in its willingness to extend a helping hand to the less fortunate. A race, like an individual, lifts itself up by lifting others up.

BOOKER T. WASHINGTON

***** *****

CHAPTER 3

***** *****

# WITH COURAGE AND FAITH

Cowards often run into the very danger they seek to avert. Don't run from anything but sin, sir, and you will be alright.

STONEWALL JACKSON

It took great courage to create America, and it requires great courage to sustain it. Freedom is never free; it is always under threat and must be preserved by each succeeding generation as an enduring legacy to the next.

In faraway places and here at home, evil is alive and well, and it must be met with righteous indignation . . . and with force. When fanaticism or despotism threatens to shred the fabric of civilized societies, brave men and women must respond. And, that's exactly what Americans do.

Public service takes many forms, of course: military, police, firefighting, and healthcare, to name but a few. But, one common trait links all those who dedicate themselves to protecting the public welfare. That trait is courage.

Andrew Jackson observed, "One man with courage is a majority." Jackson might have added that one nation, courageous, united, and free, is a glorious thing to behold.

This will remain the land of the free so long as it is the home of the brave.

ELMER DAVIS

Courage is the ladder on which all other virtues mount.

CLARE BOOTH LUCE

The future doesn't belong to the faint-hearted. It belongs to the brave.

RONALD REAGAN

What counts is not the size of the dog in the fight, but the size of the fight in the dog.

DWIGHT D. EISENHOWER

Success is not measured by what a man accomplishes, but by the opposition he has encountered, and the courage with which he maintained the struggle against overwhelming odds.

CHARLES A. LINDBERGH, JR.

All that is necessary to break the spell of inertia and frustration is this: Act as if it were impossible to fail. That is the talisman, the formula, the command of right-about-face which turns us from failure towards success.

DOROTHEA BRANDE

I would define true courage to be a perfect sensibility of the measure of danger, and a mental willingness to endure it.

WILLIAM TECUMSEH SHERMAN

Fate loves the fearless.

JAMES RUSSELL LOWELL

What a new face courage puts on everything.

RALPH WALDO EMERSON

Become so wrapped up in something that you forget to be afraid.

LADY BIRD JOHNSON

Courage is contagious.

BILLY GRAHAM

The first and great commandment is don't let them scare you.

ELMER DAVIS

Nothing is so much to be feared as fear.

HENRY DAVID THOREAU

Courage is resistance to fear, mastery of fear—not the absence of fear.

MARK TWAIN

Courage is doing what you're afraid to do. There can be no courage unless you're scared.

EDWARD RICKENBACKER

Bravery is the capacity to perform properly even when scared half to death.

OMAR BRADLEY

Bravery is being the only one who knows you are afraid.

FRANKLIN P. JONES

If fear is cultivated it will become stronger; if faith is cultivated it will achieve mastery.

JOHN PAUL JONES

Do the thing you fear and the death of fear is certain.

RALPH WALDO EMERSON

Only those who dare to fail miserably can achieve greatly.

ROBERT KENNEDY

Fill your mind with thoughts of God rather than with thoughts of fear.

NORMAN VINCENT PEALE

There's no substitute for guts. Never has been. Never will be.

BEAR BRYANT

If you want to conquer fear, don't sit home and think about it. Go out and get busy.

DALE CARNEGIE

Stop to look fear in the face.

ELEANOR ROOSEVELT

Facing it, always facing it, that's the way to get through. Face it!

JOSEPH CONRAD

Without faith nothing is possible. With it, nothing is impossible.

MARY MCLEOD BETHUNE

When we do our best, we never know what miracles await.

HELEN KELLER

The firefighters from Ladder 6 were among the first to arrive at the North Tower of the World Trade Center. They were standing together in the lobby, preparing for an 80-story climb, when they heard the sound and saw the reflection of the second explosion: the South Tower, too, had been hit. Undaunted—and with 110 pounds of gear on their backs—the six men began climbing. They made it to the 27th floor when they heard and felt a rumble like no other. At 9:50, the South Tower fell, and Battalion Chief John Jonas ordered his men to turn around and begin their descent. Jonas knew that if one tower had fallen, so, too, might the second.

The firefighters of Ladder 6 rushed down the stairs until they came upon Josephine Harris, a 60-year-old woman who, having already walked down 50 flights, was exhausted. The six firefighters stayed together, helping Harris step by agonizing step. Finally, on the fourth floor, Josephine stopped completely, and the firefighters stopped right along with her. Then the building fell.

A mountain of concrete and steel crashed around the firefighters of Ladder 6, but the stairwell offered protection. The men plunged into blackness as the floor beneath them gave way, but somehow, they were not crushed. The firefighters *and* Josephine Harris were trapped in the rubble, but miraculously they were all alive. How had they lived? The stairway of the North Tower, between the second and fourth floors, was left standing. And, because Josephine Harris had stopped there, the firefighters had been spared. Slowly but surely, six men and one woman emerged from the debris of the North Tower…alive.

Today, the men from Ladder 6 refer to Josephine Harris as their "guardian angel," and she undoubtedly feels the same way about them. And, it all happened because six brave firefighters were willing to stop and save a woman who could not save herself.

God grant me the courage not
to give up what I think is right,
even if I fear it is hopeless.

CHESTER NIMITZ

★ ★ ★ ★ ★
CHAPTER 4
★ ★ ★ ★ ★

# SERVICE
# AND
# SACRIFICE

We must be ready to dare all
for our country. For history does
not long entrust the care
of freedom to the weak
or the timid.

DWIGHT D. EISENHOWER

During the Civil War, she became known as "the Angel of the Battlefield." She was Clara Barton, a woman whose personal courage was equaled only by her fierce determination to serve. Barton once observed, "I may be compelled to face danger, but never to fear it, and while our soldiers can stand and fight, I can stand and feed and nurse them."

After the Civil War ended, Clara Barton continued a life of service. In 1881, she was the guiding force behind the formation of the American National Red Cross (that organization was modeled after the International Red Cross, which had been founded in Switzerland almost two decades before).

Throughout her life, Barton was an innovator. She observed, "I have an almost complete disregard of precedent and a faith in the possibility of something better. It irritates me to be told how things always have been done; I defy the tyranny of precedent. I cannot afford the luxury of a closed mind. I go for anything new that might improve the past."

Today, as in the days of Clara Barton, America needs men and women who are willing to serve with courage and creativity. May we, as the patriots of this generation, have ample supplies of both.

Let every nation know, whether it wishes us well or ill, we shall pay any price, bear any burden, meet any hardship, support any friend, oppose any foe, to assure the survival and success of liberty.

JOHN F. KENNEDY

In the beginning of a change, the Patriot is a scarce man, Brave, Hated, and Scorned. When his cause succeeds, however, the timid join him, for then it costs nothing to be a Patriot.

MARK TWAIN

I would rather be exposed to the inconveniences attending too much liberty than to those attending too small a degree of it.

THOMAS JEFFERSON

Those who expect to reap the blessings of freedom must undergo the fatigues of supporting it.

THOMAS PAINE

A nation is formed by the willingness of each of us to share in the responsibility for upholding the common good.

BARBARA JORDAN

No man who continues to add something to the material, intellectual, and moral well-being of the place in which he lives is ever left long without proper reward.

BOOKER T. WASHINGTON

Nobody has one chance in a billion of being thought of as great after a century has passed except those who have been servants of all.

HARRY EMERSON FOSDICK

I look upon the whole world as my fatherland. I look upon true patriotism as the brotherhood of man and the service of all to all.

HELEN KELLER

And so, my fellow Americans, ask not what your country can do for you—ask what you can do for your country.

JOHN F. KENNEDY

The individual owes the exercise of all his faculties to the service of his country.

JOHN QUINCY ADAMS

The care of human life and happiness, and not their destruction, is the first and only legitimate object of good government.

THOMAS JEFFERSON

Make yourself necessary to somebody.

RALPH WALDO EMERSON

Everybody can be great because anybody can serve.

MARTIN LUTHER KING, JR.

Service makes men and women competent.

LYMAN ABBOTT

I am only one, but still I am one; I cannot do everything, but still I can do something; I will not refuse to do the something I can do.

HELEN KELLER

Only a life lived for others is a life worthwhile.

ALBERT EINSTEIN

It is up to each of us to contribute something to this sad and wonderful world.

EVE ARDEN

Perhaps you've heard the saying "Life is a marathon, not a sprint." The same can be said for a life dedicated to serving others: like a marathon, it requires perseverance, determination, and, of course, an unending supply of energy. But sometimes, even the most dedicated public servants can find themselves exhausted by the demands of the job.

Are you discouraged? Believe in the possibility of a better tomorrow. Are you facing an uncertain future? Pray as if everything depended upon the Lord, and work as if everything depended upon you. And, remember the words of Calvin Coolidge: "Nothing in the world can take the place of persistence. Talent will not; genius will not; education will not. Persistence and determination alone are omnipotent."

Every marathon has a finish line, and so does yours. So keep putting one foot in front of the other and don't give up. Whether you realize it or not, you're up to the challenge *if* you persevere.

Some people give time,
some give money,
some their skills and
connections, some literally
give their life's blood.
But everyone has
something to give.

BARBARA BUSH

★ ★ ★ ★ ★
CHAPTER 5
★ ★ ★ ★ ★

# THROUGH CRISIS AND ADVERSITY

It is not in the still calm of life, or in repose of pacific station that great characters are formed. Great necessities call our great virtues.

ABIGAIL ADAMS

The sign on his desk read, "The Buck Stops Here." He was Harry S Truman, the feisty American president who advised, "If you can't stand the heat, get out of the kitchen." And, he spoke from experience. As commander-in-chief during the waning days of World War II, the plain-spoken Truman faced many tough decisions, and he never dodged any of them. Instead, he followed the advice of fellow Democrat Andrew Jackson, who said, "Take time to deliberate; but when the time for action arrives, stop thinking and go ahead."

Leadership should never be a popularity contest. Genuine leadership often requires tough decisions, but effective leaders are willing to sacrifice popularity for results.

Some day soon, you will face a tough decision of your own. When that day arrives, you have a choice to make: you can either do the right thing or the easy thing. Do the right thing. After all, everybody's kitchen heats up occasionally, so you might as well get used to it. And, the best way to accustom yourself to a warm kitchen is to hang in there and take the heat, knowing that every kitchen, in time, cools down. And so will yours.

Tyranny, like hell, is not easily conquered; yet, we have this consolation with us, that the harder the conflict, the more glorious the triumph.

THOMAS PAINE

There are some things you learn best in calm, and some in storm.

WILLA CATHER

There are no great men, only great challenges that ordinary men are forced by circumstance to meet.

WILLIAM F. "BULL" HALSEY

In the middle of difficulty lies opportunity.

ALBERT EINSTEIN

★　　★　　★　　★　　★

We are continually faced by great opportunities brilliantly disguised as insoluble problems.

LEE IACOCCA

Difficulties exist to be surmounted.

RALPH WALDO EMERSON

In this age, which believes that there is a short cut to everything, the greatest lesson to be learned is that the most difficult way is, in the long run, the easiest.

HENRY MILLER

Whether it's the best of times or the worst of times, it's the only time you've got.

ART BUCHWALD

Those things that hurt, instruct.

BEN FRANKLIN

Often God shuts a door in our face so that he can open the door through which he wants us to go.

CATHERINE MARSHALL

First, remember that no matter how bad a situation is, it's not as bad as you think.

COLIN POWELL

Flowers grow out of dark moments.

CORITA KENT

The country is always stronger than we know in our most worried moments.

E. B. WHITE

God will not look you over for medals, degrees, or diplomas, but for scars.

ELBERT HUBBARD

'Tis easy enough to be pleasant, when life flows along like a song. But the man worthwhile is the one who will smile when everything goes dead wrong.

ELLA WHEELER WILCOX

To be tested is good. The challenged life may be the best therapist.

GAIL SHEEHY

God's signs are not always the ones we look for. We learn in tragedy that His purposes are not always our own. Yet the prayers of private suffering, whether in our homes or in this great cathedral, are known and heard, and understood.

GEORGE W. BUSH

Although the world is full of suffering, it is also full of overcoming it.

HELEN KELLER

What's right about America is that although we have a mess of problems, we have a great capacity, intellect, and resources to do something about them.

HENRY FORD II

The lowest ebb is at the turn of the tide.

HENRY WADSWORTH LONGFELLOW

Troubles are often the tools
by which God fashions us
for better things.

HENRY WARD BEECHER

Great crises produce great men and great deeds of courage.

JOHN F. KENNEDY

It is by presence of mind in untried emergencies that the native metal of a man is tested.

JAMES RUSSELL LOWELL

I am not afraid of storms, for I am learning how to sail my ship.

LOUISA MAY ALCOTT

The Reverend Martin Luther King, Jr. once observed, "The ultimate measure of a man is not where he stands in moments of comfort, but where he stands at times of challenge and controversy." Dr. King spoke from personal experience. During the turbulent 1960's, he fought the injustice of American segregation and became an example of strength and courage to a nation that desperately needed both.

Dr. King observed, "Everybody can be great because everybody can serve." If you'd like to achieve enduring greatness in *your* world, find a place to serve, and get busy. Be willing to offer your service in times of comfort *and* in times of challenge. You'll discover that greatness is available to anyone who is willing to pitch in and work for the common good. And, as Martin Luther King, Jr. proved once and for all, the greater your service, the greater your legacy.

When a great ship cuts through the sea, the waters are always stirred and troubled. And, our ship is moving, moving through troubled waters, toward new and better shores.

LYNDON BAINES JOHNSON

★ ★ ★ ★ ★

CHAPTER 6

★ ★ ★ ★ ★

# FIGHTING FOR FREEDOM AND JUSTICE

Freedom! No word was ever spoken that held out greater hope, demanded greater sacrifice, needed more to be nurtured, blessed more the giver, cursed more its destroyer, or came closer to being God's will on earth. And, I think that's worth fighting for.

OMAR BRADLEY

In 1944, world freedom hung in the balance as American soldiers and their allies prepared for the largest amphibious attack in history. Hitler's troops had dominated Europe and had occupied France; now, the Nazis were systematically murdering millions of innocent civilians. On June 6, the Allied Forces, under the leadership of General Dwight Eisenhower, began the liberation of Europe by launching Operation Overlord, an invasion that included over 5,000 ships, 10,000 airplanes, and 150,000 service men and women.

Most of the young soldiers who waded onto the beaches of Normandy that morning were under twenty years of age; they carried eighty pounds of equipment through the surf as they sprinted into a firestorm of German bullets. And, once the Allied soldiers had scrambled across 200 yards of unprotected beach to reach the base of the Normandy cliffs, they then climbed to the top where they engaged and defeated the heavily fortified Germans.

D-Day, June 6, 1944 was a day that changed the course of history. On that day, 4,000 Allied soldiers died for the cause of freedom. May we remember them always, as we do all the heroes and patriots who paid for the American Dream with their blood and their tears. And, may *we* never stop fighting in defense of the liberties they held dear.

★　　★　　★　　★　　★

We highly resolve that this nation, under God, shall have a new birth of freedom, and that government of the people, by the people, for the people, shall not perish from the earth.

ABRAHAM LINCOLN

The best energies of my life have been spent in endeavoring to establish and perpetuate the blessings of free government.

ANDREW JOHNSON

All men are born free and equal, and have certain natural, essential, and unalienable rights.

THE CONSTITUTION OF MASSACHUSETTS

In the truest sense, freedom cannot be bestowed; it must be achieved.

FRANKLIN D. ROOSEVELT

We know the best way to enhance freedom in other lands is to demonstrate here that our democratic system is worthy of emulation.

JIMMY CARTER

In the long history of the world, only a few generations have been granted the role of defending freedom in its hour of maximum danger. I do not shrink from this responsibility—I welcome it.

JOHN F. KENNEDY

None who have always been free can understand the terrible, fascinating power of the hope of freedom to those who are not free.

PEARL BUCK

Freedom lies in being bold.

ROBERT FROST

Justice, sir, is the great interest of man on earth. It is the ligament which holds civilized beings and civilized nations together.

DANIEL WEBSTER

Justice is the desired end of government. It is the desired end of civil liberty. It ever has been and ever will be pursued until it be obtained, or until liberty be lost in the pursuit.

JAMES MADISON

The answer to injustice is not to silence the critic but to end the injustice.

PAUL ROBESON

I believe in one God, and no more, and I hope for happiness beyond this life. I believe in the equality of man; and I believe that religious duties consist in doing justice, loving mercy, and endeavoring to make our fellow creatures happy.

THOMAS PAINE

Man's capacity for justice makes democracy possible, but man's inclination to injustice makes democracy necessary.

REINHOLD NEIBUHR

Since when do you have to agree with people to defend them from injustice?

LILLIAN HELLMAN

A government of laws, not of men.

JOHN ADAMS

I hope ever to see America among the foremost nations in examples of justice and tolerance.

GEORGE WASHINGTON

True patriotism hates injustice in its own land more than anywhere else.

CLARENCE DARROW

It is the spirit and not the form of law that keeps justice alive.

EARL WARREN

You know that being an American is more than a matter of where your parents came from. It is a belief that all men are created free and equal and that everyone deserves an even break. It is a respect for the dignity of all men and women without regard to race, creed, or color.

HARRY S TRUMAN

Man is unjust, but God is just, and finally justice triumphs.

HENRY WADSWORTH LONGFELLOW

Standing for right when it is
unpopular is a true test
of moral character.

MARGARET CHASE SMITH

No man is above the law and no man is below it; nor do we ask any man's permission when we ask him to obey it.

THEODORE ROOSEVELT

Justice delayed is democracy denied.

ROBERT KENNEDY

Generosity is the flower of justice.

NATHANIEL HAWTHORNE

We will not be satisfied until justice rolls down like waters and righteousness like a mighty stream.

MARTIN LUTHER KING, JR.

Abraham Lincoln's words still ring true: "No man is good enough to govern another man without the other's consent." But across the globe, tyranny and oppression still grip the lives of far too many innocent men, women, and children. When people anywhere are denied their freedoms, people everywhere are threatened. And so it is that American men and women must, on occasion, travel far beyond our borders to protect the lives and liberties of foreign citizens.

Perhaps you have sometimes taken America's freedoms for granted. If so, you're not alone. In a land so richly blessed, we can easily forget how hard our forefathers struggled to earn the blessings that we enjoy today. But, we must never forget, and we must never become complacent.

In America, no man governs alone. We the people make the laws, enforce the laws, and change the laws when those laws need changing. For these liberties, we must thank those who have gone before us. And the best way to say "thank you" for our blessings is to defend them, whatever the cost.

I know not what course others
may take, but as for me,
give me liberty or
give me death.

PATRICK HENRY

# CHAPTER 7

# WITH A SPIRIT OF OPTIMISM

The only limit to our realization of tomorrow will be our doubts of today. Let us move forward with strong and active faith.

FRANKLIN D. ROOSEVELT

The Declaration of Independence contains the words that are so familiar and so reassuring: "life, liberty, and the pursuit of happiness." And, because we are free to pursue our hopes and dreams, we Americans are a nation of optimists. America was built by men and women who possessed mountain-moving faith: faith in themselves, faith in each other, faith in their nation, and faith in their God. In the future, America will be sustained by men and women of faith and optimism.

John F. Kennedy was correct when he observed, "The American, by nature, is optimistic. He is experimental, an inventor and a builder who builds best when called upon to build greatly."

Our nation steadfastly preserves the rights of the naysayers to complain to their hearts' content, but we seldom follow them. Instead, we find leaders who can help us visualize—and realize—the possibilities of America.

Do you seek to be a leader here in the land of the free and the home of the brave? If so, be forewarned: pessimists need not apply. America was founded by optimists, built by optimists, and preserved by optimists. And, for that matter, America is populated by a people who are, by and large, optimistic to the core. We Americans can do great things precisely because we think we can. And, because we think we can, we're right.

Be hopeful! For tomorrow has never happened before.

ROBERT SCHULLER

Go forward confidently, energetically attacking problems, expecting favorable outcomes.

NORMAN VINCENT PEALE

A pessimist is one who makes difficulties of his opportunities; an optimist is one who makes opportunities of his difficulties.

HARRY S TRUMAN

I can do all things through Him who strengthens me.

PHILIPPIANS 4:13 NASB

Perpetual optimism is a force multiplier.

COLIN POWELL

Think positively and masterfully, with confidence and faith, and life becomes more secure, more fraught with action, richer in achievement and experience.

EDDIE RICKENBACKER

Without faith nothing is possible. With it, nothing is impossible.

MARY MCLEOD BETHUNE

Write on your heart that every day is the best day of the year.

RALPH WALDO EMERSON

In the time of your life, live—so that in the good time there shall be no ugliness or death for yourself or for any life your life touches. Seek goodness everywhere, and where it is found, bring it out of its hiding place and let it be free and unashamed.

WILLIAM SAROYAN

I've never seen a monument erected to a pessimist.

PAUL HARVEY

Don't bring negatives to my door.

MAYA ANGELOU

No pessimist ever discovered the secrets of the stars or sailed to an uncharted land, or opened a new heaven to the human spirit.

HELEN KELLER

Positive anything is better than negative nothing.

ELBERT HUBBARD

The sun shines not on us, but in us.

JOHN MUIR

Far away in the sunshine are my highest inspirations. I may not reach them, but I can look up and see the beauty, believe in them and try to follow where they lead.

LOUISA MAY ALCOTT

The more you praise and celebrate your life, the more there is in life to celebrate.

OPRAH WINFREY

A positive mind tunes in to other positive minds.

NAPOLEON HILL

Neil Armstrong served his country in Korea and became a civilian test pilot *before* he joined NASA as an astronaut in 1962. As commander of the Apollo 11, he made history when he became the first man to set foot on the moon. On July 20, 1969, all the world marveled as Armstrong's landing craft came to rest on the lunar surface. And, shortly thereafter, Armstrong took "one small step for a man, one giant leap for mankind." When questioned later about his fears of not returning from the moon, Neil Armstrong replied, "We planned for every negative contingency, but we expected success."

If you would like to watch *your* life blast off, take this hint from NASA: plan for the worst, but don't expect it. Don't ignore your fears, but don't be ruled by them, either. And, when it comes to your expectations, visualize success and think optimistically. When you do, the sky is truly the limit.

# Change your thoughts and you change your world.

## NORMAN VINCENT PEALE

★ ★ ★ ★ ★
CHAPTER 8
★ ★ ★ ★ ★

# SERVING
# WITH
# INTEGRITY

In matters of style,
swim with the current;
in matters of principle,
stand like a rock.

THOMAS JEFFERSON

Thomas Paine correctly observed, "Character is much easier kept than recovered." Character is built slowly over a lifetime. It is the sum of every right decision, every honest word, every noble thought, and every heartfelt prayer. It is forged on the anvil of honorable work and polished by the twin virtues of generosity and humility.

Character is a precious thing—difficult to build but easy to tear down. As Americans who value honor and truth, we must seek to live each day with discipline, integrity, and faith. When we do, integrity becomes a habit . . . and God smiles upon us and upon our nation.

Try not to become men of success. Rather, become men of value.

ALBERT EINSTEIN

We are effective only when we have integrity, when our actions are in line with our values.

STEPHEN COVEY

Honor is self-esteem made visible in action.

AYN RAND

Character is like a tree and reputation like its shadow. The shadow is what we think; the tree is the real thing.

ABRAHAM LINCOLN

Character is power.

BOOKER T. WASHINGTON

Character is what you are in the dark.

DWIGHT L. MOODY

Character is not revealed when life shows its best side, but when it shows its worst.

FULTON J. SHEEN

Character is a by-product.
It is produced in the great
manufacture of daily duty.

WOODROW WILSON

Human happiness and moral duty are inseparably connected.

GEORGE WASHINGTON

Character and personal force are the only investments that are worth anything.

WALT WHITMAN

I care not what others think of what I do, but I care very much about what I think of what I do. That is character!

THEODORE ROOSEVELT

The integrity of the upright shall guide them.

PROVERBS 11:3 KJV

The force of character is cumulative.

RALPH WALDO EMERSON

Endeavor to live so that when you die, even the undertaker will be sorry.

MARK TWAIN

You can easily judge the character of others by how they treat those who can do nothing for them or to them.

MALCOLM FORBES

We often pray for purity, unselfishness, for the highest qualities of character, and forget that these things cannot be given but must be earned.

LYMAN ABBOTT

All sober inquirers after truth, ancient and modern, pagan and Christian, have declared that the happiness of man, as well as his dignity, consists in virtue.

JOHN ADAMS

Happiness is not the end of life; character is.

HENRY WARD BEECHER

Of all the properties which belong to honorable men, not one is so highly prized as that of character.

HENRY CLAY

We do not need more knowledge; we need more character!

CALVIN COOLIDGE

No amount of ability is of the slightest avail without honor.

ANDREW CARNEGIE

Character is the result of two things—mental attitude and the way we spend our time.

ELBERT HUBBARD

Character building begins in infancy and ends in death.

ELEANOR ROOSEVELT

Character builds slowly, but it can be torn down with incredible swiftness.

FAITH BALDWIN

Ralph Waldo Emerson could have been speaking about both individuals *and* governments when he warned, "Nothing can bring you peace but the triumph of principles." Sometimes, however, principles are easier to talk about than they are to live by. In trying times, we may be tempted to take shortcuts, but, as Beverly Sills reminds us, "There are no shortcuts to any place worth going." When facing difficult times, what's required is character, and lots of it.

None other than the father of our country, George Washington, wrote, "The most enviable of all titles: an honest man." Mr. Washington's words prove once and for all that father indeed knows best: Character counts. It did in Washington's time; it does now, and it always will.

Character, not circumstances,
makes the man.

BOOKER T. WASHINGTON

★ ★ ★ ★ ★
CHAPTER 9
★ ★ ★ ★ ★

# THE COURAGE
# TO
# PERSEVERE

The first requisite for success is the ability to apply your physical and mental energies to one problem incessantly without growing weary.

THOMAS EDISON

America was not built by the faint of heart. To the contrary, the men and women who built this nation were resolute in their determination to succeed, and we should be, too. Dwight D. Eisenhower observed, "What counts is not the size of the dog in the fight, but the size of the fight in the dog." His words still ring true. In America, success is often the result of little more than a good idea and a persevering spirit. Those who succeed here are those with the endurance and will to persevere.

Do you seek a magical solution to your problems? If so, don't go looking in the local magic shop; instead look inside yourself and bring forth the inner strength to keep working even when you'd rather quit. Find the courage to stand firm in the face of adversity. Don't back up and don't back down. Because, here in America, courage and perseverance have a way of making problems disappear . . . unless you disappear first.

All great masters are chiefly distinguished by the power of adding a second, a third, and perhaps a fourth step in a continuous line. Many a man had taken the first step. With every additional step you enhance immensely the value of your first.

RALPH WALDO EMERSON

There is no royal road to anything. Do one thing at a time and all things in succession. That which grows slowly, endures.

JOSIAH GILBERT HOLLAND

When you get into a tight place and everything goes against you, till it seems as though you could not hang on a minute longer, never give up then, for that is just the place and the time the tide will turn.

HARRIET BEECHER STOWE

You do what you can for as long as you can, and when you finally can't, you do the next best thing. You back up but you don't give up.

CHUCK YEAGER

If I had permitted my failures to discourage me, I cannot see any way in which I would ever have made progress.

CALVIN COOLIDGE

About all I did was stick with it.

BEAR BRYANT

It's not that I'm so smart; it's just that I stay with problems longer.

ALBERT EINSTEIN

Always bear in mind that your own resolution to succeed is more important than any one thing.

ABRAHAM LINCOLN

Keep your mind on your objective, and persist until you succeed.

W. CLEMENT STONE

Energy and persistence alter all things.

BEN FRANKLIN

One may walk over the highest mountain one step at a time.

JOHN WANAMAKER

Genius may conceive, but patient labor must consummate.

HORACE MANN

First, one must endure.

ERNEST HEMINGWAY

Effort only fully releases its reward after a person refuses to quit.

NAPOLEON HILL

That which we persist in doing becomes easier—not that the nature of the task has changed, but our ability has increased.

RALPH WALDO EMERSON

Be like a postage stamp: Stick to one thing till you get there.

JOSH BILLINGS

Those who hope in the LORD will renew their strength. They will soar on wings like eagles; they will run and not grow weary, they will walk and not be faint.

ISAIAH 40:31 NIV

Big shots are only little shots who kept on shooting.

HARVEY MACKAY

There is no chance, no destiny,
no fate, that can hinder or
control the firm resolve of
a determined soul.

ELLA WHEELER WILCOX

There is no failure except in no longer trying.

ELBERT HUBBARD

Success seems to be connected with action. Successful men keep moving. They make mistakes, but they don't quit.

CONRAD HILTON

Nothing in the world can take the place of persistence. Talent will not; genius will not; education will not. Persistence and determination alone are omnipotent.

CALVIN COOLIDGE

Little strokes fell great oaks.

BEN FRANKLIN

Elbert Hubbard observed, "When troubles arise, wise men go to their work." Easier said than done. During difficult times, we are tempted to complain, to worry, to blame, and to do little else. Usually, complaints and worries change nothing; intelligent work, on the other hand, changes everything for the better.

In times of danger and adversity, even the most dedicated men and women can, for a while, lose hope. But, we must never abandon our hopes altogether. America was built upon the hopes and dreams of its citizens; if we are to build a better nation for our children and theirs, we must continue to believe in—and work for—a brighter future.

Undeniably, America faces serious challenges both at home and abroad. The world, it seems, is an ever-more-dangerous place, and solutions seem harder than ever to come by. But, even in a dangerous world, we must not give in; we must persevere. What's required is a combination of faith, work, wisdom, courage, and teamwork. Then, when we stand united and face the dangers of the world with open eyes and courageous hearts, no adversary on earth can defeat us.

Courage and perseverance
have a magical talisman,
before which difficulties
disappear and obstacles
vanish into thin air.

JOHN QUINCY ADAMS

★ ★ ★ ★ ★

# CHAPTER 10

★ ★ ★ ★ ★

# THE FAMILY ALSO SERVES

Families are where
our nation finds hope,
where dreams take wing.

GEORGE W. BUSH

★　　★　　★　　★　　★

I f you've made the choice to lead a life of service, whether in the military or as a civilian, whether in the government sector or the private, you know that your family pays a price for the sacrifices you make. If you work long hours, your family feels your absence. If you travel far from home, your family waits anxiously for your return. If you place your life in danger, your family wonders and worries . . . constantly.

On the pages that follow, we pay tribute to the women and the men and the boys and the girls who keep the home fires burning at *your* house. A grateful nation also honors its families because families also serve.

Whatever the times, one thing will never change: Fathers and mothers, if you have children, they must come first. Your success as a family, our success as a society, depends not on what happens in the White House, but on what happens inside your house.

BARBARA BUSH

It takes a heap of livin' in a house to make it home.

EDGAR A. GUEST

…these should learn first of all to put their religion into practice by caring for their own family….

1 TIMOTHY 5:4 NIV

Money can build or buy a house. Add love to that, and you have a home. Add God to that, and you have a temple. You have "a little colony of the kingdom of heaven."

ANNE ORTLAND

We must strengthen our commitment to model strong families ourselves, to live by godly priorities in a culture where self so often supersedes commitment to others. And, as we not only model but assertively reach out to help others, we must realize that even huge societal problems are solved one person at a time.

CHUCK COLSON

Home, in one form or another, is the great objective of life.

JOSIAH GILBERT HOLLAND

When you look at your life, the greatest happiness is family business.

JOYCE BROTHERS

Keep your family from the abominable practice of backbiting.

THE OLD FARMER'S ALMANAC, 1811

You have to love a nation that celebrates its independence every July 4, not with a parade of guns, tanks, and soldiers who file by the White House in a show of strength and muscle, but with family picnics where kids throw Frisbees, the potato salad gets iffy, and the flies die from happiness. You may think you have overeaten, but it is patriotism.

ERMA BOMBECK

The happiest moments of my life have been spent in the bosom of my family.

THOMAS JEFFERSON

The only true source of meaning in life is found in love for God and his son Jesus Christ, and love for mankind, beginning with our own families.

JAMES DOBSON

Apart from religious influence, the family is the most important influence of society.

BILLY GRAHAM

Every kingdom divided against itself will be ruined, and every city or household divided against itself will not stand.

MATTHEW 12:25 NIV

Having family responsibilities and concerns just has to make you a more understanding person.

SANDRA DAY O'CONNOR

The family. We are a strange little band of characters trudging through life sharing diseases, toothpaste, coveting one another's desserts, hiding shampoo, borrowing money, locking each other out of rooms, loving, laughing, defending, and trying to figure out the common thread that bound us all together.

ERMA BOMBECK

A family ought to be a lot more than a collection of mutual needs. It ought to be fun.

ART LINKLETTER

A home is a place where we find direction.

GIGI GRAHAM TCHIVIDJIAN

He blesses the home of the righteous.

PROVERBS 3:33 NIV

George Washington, in a letter to his wife, Martha, wrote, "I should enjoy more real happiness in one month with you at home than I have the most distant prospect of finding abroad, if my stay were to be seven times seven years." Family-loving Americans agree. Home is not only where the heart is; it is also where the happiness is.

Your family is your most prized earthly possession; it is a priceless gift from God. Treasure it and protect it. That little band of men, women, kids, and babies is a priceless treasure on temporary loan from the Father above. Give thanks to the Giver for the gift of family . . .and act accordingly.

No nation can be destroyed
while it possesses
a good home life.

JOSIAH GILBERT HOLLAND

★ ★ ★ ★ ★
CHAPTER 11
★ ★ ★ ★ ★

# THE ULTIMATE SACRIFICE

The greatest use of a life is
to spend it for something that
will outlast it.

WILLIAM JAMES

At the National Cathedral, on September 14, 2001, George W. Bush spoke to a nation in mourning: "As we have been assured, neither death nor life, not angels nor principalities nor powers, not things present nor things to come, nor height nor depth, can separate us from God's love. May He bless the souls of the departed. May He comfort our own. And may He always guide our country. God bless America."

Each generation must learn this lesson again: The fight for freedom is not a dress rehearsal; it takes place in a real world with real enemies and real dangers. And, in the struggle to protect our families and preserve our liberties, some men and women must pay the ultimate price. The United States of America owes its greatest debt to these heroes.

To those of us who are left behind, even the most heartfelt words of consolation may ring hollow. But, the fact remains that Americans who give their lives in the service of their fellow citizens are heroes of the first order. May God give them eternal peace, and may we keep their memories alive in our hearts today and forevermore.

We have enjoyed so much freedom for so long that we are perhaps in danger of forgetting how much blood it cost to establish the Bill of Rights.

FELIX FRANKFURTER

HERE RESTS IN HONORED
GLORY AN AMERICAN
SOLDIER KNOWN
BUT TO GOD.

INSCRIPTION ON THE TOMB OF THE
UNKNOWN SOLDIER AT ARLINGTON
NATIONAL CEMETERY

If it be the pleasure of Heaven that my country shall require the poor offering of my life, the victim shall be ready, at the appointed hour of sacrifice, come when that hour may. But while I do live, let me have a country that is free.

JOHN ADAMS

Though I walk through the valley of the shadow of death, I will fear no evil: for thou art with me.

PSALM 23:4 KJV

Democracy is never a final achievement. It is a call to untiring effort, to continual sacrifice and to the willingness, if necessary, to die in its defense.

JOHN F. KENNEDY

TO THE MEMORY OF THE
GALLANT MEN HERE,
ENTOMBED. AND THEIR
SHIPMATES WHO GAVE
THEIR LIVES IN ACTION
ON DECEMBER 7, 1941.

INSCRIPTION ON U.S.S. ARIZONA MEMORIAL,
PEARL HARBOR

The cost of freedom is always high, but Americans have always paid it.

JOHN F. KENNEDY

War drew us from our homeland in the sunlit springtime of our youth. Those who did not come back alive remain in perpetual springtime—forever young—and a part of them is with us always.

ANONYMOUS

I pray that our Heavenly Father may assuage the anguish of your bereavement, and leave you only the cherished memory of the loved and lost, and the solemn pride that must be yours, to have laid so costly a sacrifice upon the altar of Freedom.

ABRAHAM LINCOLN

Blessed are they that mourn, for they will be comforted.

MATTHEW 5:4 NIV

Uncommon Valor was a Common Virtue

FLEET ADM. CHESTER W. NIMITZ

FROM THE INSCRIPTION ON

THE IWO JIMA MEMORIAL

We must be ready to dare all for our country. For history does not long entrust the care of freedom to the weak or the timid.

DWIGHT D. EISENHOWER

Those who won our independence believed liberty to be the secret of happiness and courage to be the secret of liberty.

LOUIS D. BRANDEIS

This will remain the land of the free only so long as it is the home of the brave.

ELMER DAVIS

★　　★　　★　　★　　★　　135

We Americans understand freedom; we have earned it, we have lived for it, and we have died for it. This nation and its people are freedom's models in a searching world. We can be freedom's missionaries in a doubting world.

BARRY GOLDWATER

On the morning of September 11, United Flight 93 sat on the runway for forty minutes before finally taking off from the Newark airport. That delay may have saved hundreds of American lives. Without that delay, the plane's passengers might never have learned of the attacks on the World Trade Center. But, because of the delay, the men and women on board Flight 93 had sufficient time to learn the full details of the terrorist atrocities. As the hijackers flew toward Washington, D.C., a small group of heroes entered the cockpit and brought down the plane.

The names of the heroes onboard Flight 93 are now a permanent part of American history: Beemer, Bingham, Bradshaw, Burnett, and Glick, along with their fellow crew members and passengers. And, the story of their heroism reminds us that none of us know when *we* may be called upon to fight for the freedom and safety of our fellow citizens. If that day ever comes, may we, too, answer the call with courage and faith.

Freedom is still expensive. It still costs money. It still costs blood. It still calls for courage and endurance, not only in soldiers, but in every man and woman who is free and who is determined to remain free.

HARRY S TRUMAN

★ ★ ★ ★ ★

CHAPTER 12

★ ★ ★ ★ ★

# ONE NATION UNDER GOD

And to the same Divine Author of every good and perfect gift, we are indebted for all those privileges and advantages, religious as well as civil, which are so richly enjoyed in this favored land.

JAMES MADISON

The words are familiar to every school-child: "One nation, under God . . . ." And, if we sit down and begin counting the blessings that God has bestowed upon our nation, the list is improbably long. At the top of that list, of course, is the priceless gift of freedom: the freedom to live, vote, work, and worship without fear. God has also blessed America with unsurpassed material wealth; we are, in fact, the most prosperous nation in the history of humanity.

To those to whom much is given, much is expected, and so it is with America. We are the world's superpower, and as such, we have profound responsibilities to our own citizens and, to a lesser extent, to those who live beyond our borders. The challenges are great, and no single individual, no matter how wise, can chart the proper course for our nation. But, *we the people*—under God and respectful of His commandments—*can* join together to protect and preserve our nation and, in doing so, give protection and hope to freedom-loving people around the globe.

America has been called "the land of our fathers." May we also make it the land of our Father . . . and may we make the Father proud.

Every thinking man, when he thinks, realizes that the teachings of the Bible are so interwoven and entwined with our whole civic and social life that it would be literally, I do not mean figuratively, but literally, impossible for us to figure what that loss would be if these teachings were removed. We would lose all the standards by which we now judge both public and private morals; all the standards towards which we, with more or less resolution, strive to raise ourselves.

THEODORE ROOSEVELT

God is going to reveal to us things he never revealed before *if* we put our hands in His. No books ever go into my laboratory. The thing I am to do and the way of doing it are revealed to me. I never have to grope for methods. The method is revealed to me the moment I am inspired to create something new. Without God to draw aside the curtain I would be helpless.

GEORGE WASHINGTON CARVER

The Almighty God has blessed our land in many ways. He has given our people stout hearts and strong arms with which to strike mighty blows for freedom and truth. He has given to our country a faith which has become the hope of all peoples in an anguished world.

FRANKLIN D. ROOSEVELT

If my people who are called
by my name, will humble
themselves and pray and seek
my face and turn from their
wicked ways, then will I hear
from heaven and will forgive
their sin and will heal
their land.

2 CHRONICLES 7:14 NIV

My God! How little do my
countrymen know what
precious blessings they are
in possession of, and which
no other people
on earth enjoy!

THOMAS JEFFERSON

It is the duty of nations, as well as of men, to base their dependence upon the overruling power of God and to recognize the sublime truth announced in the Holy Scriptures and proven by all history, that those nations only are blessed whose God is Lord.

ABRAHAM LINCOLN

Freedom is not a gift bestowed upon us by other men, but a right that belongs to us by the laws of God and nature. The pleasures of this world are rather from God's goodness than our own merit. Whoever shall introduce into the public affairs the principles of primitive Christianity will change the face of the world.

BEN FRANKLIN

If we make religion our business, God will make it our blessedness.

JOHN ADAMS

The God who gave us life gave us liberty at the same time.

THOMAS JEFFERSON

I shall know but one country. The ends I aim at shall be my country's, my God's, and Truth's.

DANIEL WEBSTER

This, then, is the state of the union: free and restless, growing, and full of hope. So it was in the beginning. So it shall always be, while God is willing, and we are strong enough to keep the faith.

LYNDON BAINES JOHNSON

We have staked the future of all our political institutions upon the capacity of mankind for self-government, upon the capacity of each and all of us to govern ourselves, to control ourselves, to sustain ourselves according to the Ten Commandments of God.

JAMES MADISON

I have been driven many times to my knees by the overwhelming conviction that I had nowhere else to go. My own wisdom, and that of all about me, seemed insufficient for the day.

ABRAHAM LINCOLN

No people can be bound to acknowledge and adore the Invisible Hand which conducts the affairs of men more than the people of the United States.

GEORGE WASHINGTON

Our institutions of freedom will not survive unless they are constantly replenished by the faith that gave them birth.

JOHN FOSTER DULLES

You have rights antecedent to all earthly governments; rights that cannot be repeated or retrained by human laws; rights derived from the Great Legislator of the Universe.

JOHN ADAMS

Since its earliest days, America has been a nation led by god-fearing men and women. The founding fathers were quick to ensure freedom of religion for Americans of all faiths. And, the Word of God, as found in both the Old Testament and the New, has been— and continues to be—an integral part of American life. In the New Testament, Jesus instructs His followers that, "The greatest among you will be your servant" (Matthew 23:10 NIV). Thankfully, Americans of every generation have heeded these words. The spirit of unselfish service is woven into the very fabric of American life.

We owe our undying gratitude to the men and women who serve in the military, in government, in healthcare, and in the helping professions. Without them, the promise of this great nation would remain unfulfilled. With them, the America

Let us go forth asking His help and His blessing, but knowing that here on earth, God's work must truly be our own.

JOHN F. KENNEDY

★ ★ ★ ★ ★

## CHAPTER 13

★ ★ ★ ★ ★

# A GIFT FOR OUR CHILDREN

A compassionate government keeps faith with the trust of the people and cherishes the future of their children. Through compassion for the plight of one individual, government fulfills its purpose as the servant of all people.

LYNDON BAINES JOHNSON

Thomas Paine wrote, "If there must be trouble, let it be in my day, that my child may have peace." Parents and grandparents of every generation agree. As protectors of the next generation, we live as much for our children and grandchildren as we do for ourselves. If troubles must be visited upon our land, we, as responsible adults, must meet those troubles now with all the strength we can muster. To do otherwise is unthinkable.

Jimmy Carter observed, "Many of the most highly publicized events of my presidency are not nearly as memorable or significant in my life as fishing with my daddy." Those of us who, like Mr. Carter, possess happy memories of parents and grandparents owe a profound debt to those who have gone before. We repay that debt, not to our forefathers, but to our children. May God give us the strength to repay it in full.

A baby is God's opinion that life should go on.

CARL SANDBURG

We need to teach the next generation of children from Day One that they are responsible for their lives. Mankind's greatest gift, also its greatest curse, is that we have free choice. We can make our choices built from love or from fear.

ELIZABETH ·KÜBLER-ROSS

Each child is an adventure into a better life— an opportunity to change the old pattern and make it new.

HUBERT H. HUMPHREY

Be careful with truth towards children; to a child, the parent or teacher is the representative of justice.

MARGARET FULLER

America's future will be determined by the home and the school. The child becomes largely what it is taught; hence, we must watch what we teach it and how we live before it.

JANE ADDAMS

The Creator has given to us the awesome responsibility of representing him to our children. Our heavenly Father is a God of unlimited love, and our children must become acquainted with his mercy and tenderness through our own love toward them.

JAMES DOBSON

Children miss nothing in sizing up their parents. If you are only half convinced of your beliefs, they will quickly discern that fact. Any ethical weak spot, any indecision on your part, will be incorporated and then magnified in your sons and daughters. Their faith or faithlessness will be a reflection of our own.

JAMES DOBSON

    155

Our reliance is in the love of liberty. Our defense is in the preservation of the spirit which prizes liberty as the heritage of all men, in all lands, everywhere.

ABRAHAM LINCOLN

We take the stars from heaven, the red from our mother country, separating it by white stripes, thus showing that we have separated from her, and the white stripes shall go down to posterity, representing our liberty.

GEORGE WASHINGTON

We need an America with the wisdom of experience. But we must not let America grow old in Spirit.

HUBERT H. HUMPHREY

"The American Dream": this phrase is unique to the nation we call home. Nowhere do we hear the phrase the "Russian Dream," even though Russia is a nation struggling to become a working democracy. We don't talk about the "Chinese Dream," the "Mexican Dream," the "Indian Dream," or the "French Dream." In many places around the globe, democracies rule, but no place on earth is like America. No nation offers more opportunities and more personal freedoms; no nation offers more possibilities and more fresh starts than the good old USA. America is a land tailor-made for dreamers, especially those willing to work for their dreams.

Americans of this generation have a grand opportunity: we can leave an enduring legacy to our children. That legacy, of course, is a nation strong and free, and we, as protectors of liberty's flame, must do our utmost to leave to the next generation a better nation than the one we received from the last. May our legacy be worthy of those who sacrificed so much to ensure that the Dream will never die. And may God Bless America forever.